NAME

ADDRESS

contents

PAGE NUMBER	SUBJECT

crownpublishing.com
clarksonpotter.com

ISBN 978-1-9848-2559-9

Design by Marysarah Quinn

PRINTED IN CHINA